The Luminary

The Luminary

KIMIA MADANI

**THOUGHT
CATALOG**
Books

BROOKLYN, NY

THOUGHT CATALOG Books

Published by Thought Catalog Books, a division of The Thought & Expression Co., Williamsburg, Brooklyn. Founded in 2010, Thought Catalog is a website and imprint dedicated to your ideas and stories. We publish fiction and non-fiction from emerging and established writers across all genres. For general information and submissions: manuscripts@thoughtcatalog.com.

First edition, 2017

ISBN: 978-1945796371

Printed and bound in the United States.

10 9 8 7 6 5 4 3 2 1

lu·mi·nar·y | \ ˈlü-mə-ˌner-ē\

1. a body that gives light; especially : one of the celestial bodies.
2. In astrology, one of the brightest celestial objects, such as the sun or moon.

CONTENTS

Map of a Human Being

Mythwork

Keeping the Light

Map of a Human Being

Empty Spaces

I am fascinated by
emptiness, by the sheer
density of it—all those atoms
fitted together within empty
space, strung along
between the
bones.

Intergalactic

One look, and you had all of the
galaxies within me
singing

Map of a Human Being

Crystals that glitter when placed upon faded maps;
stretches of white world expanse going on and on
into strange emptinesses I no longer fear.

My heart is a compass, its surface cracked.
The brink: It wavers like a tightrope, blank and empty,
wind-buzzed. My soul is another story entirely—

an iridescent cloak that has been laid flat upon the world.
Chunks of mountain press through, still, and up into the night.
I wear the sky like a great overcoat. My soul goes on and on.

On.

Alchemy

False like pyrite, your smile winks like the glittering
at the bottom of a well; false teeth catch on chapped lips.
I am not gold
but being turned into it.

The act: The lovely, blank-eyed in-betweens.
No, I am an entirely different sort of thing; draped in lace dresses,
shimmering sequined cloth. Winged chiffon, thin as gossamer.

I clear my throat—faux furs and velvet, luxurious silks—
rubbing my gums, spitting false beneath the light.
I wear glitter on my skin,

peck the false-eyed crescent moon. Transformation, a lost art.
I fly into wild spiraling depressions, I'm certain I'm disliked.
But somehow I can't make myself

fit
Shrink down between the lines.
No matter: You are not Midas, and I am not gold.

Permission Slip from the Universe

Why must I be granted permission
to be cosmic? Why the constant wearing of different
selves like a series of coats to tug on?

Braiding my heartbreak, the ever-rippling tides
of your mistakes. C'mon, make 'em pretty.

The sunlight is deafening
as we cut through the smoke. And at age 25,
life is both crueler and fuller than I have ever known it to be.

Watch: My mind unspools itself like an old VHS tape—
battered thoughts tangling up in one another. All caught up

in the reckless outpour of our over-saturated emoticons,
sunny, thick and hazy as an Instagram filter
over my mind's eye.

Shrapnel

I know I was too much for you
I was too much for myself
I spent the days dozing on a pyre of self-hate
wondering why no one would ever stay
Immeasurably drifting, my past
a battleground; not for the faint of heart
Blasted shrapnel embedded in each childhood memory
doesn't make for easy dinnertime conversation
Your words cut deeper than mere surface wounds
They cut down to the very bone

Adrift

I would never need what you could not give
What was always mine, not yours
I will not always be adrift
Lost in a sea of myself; littered,
another victim of the shipwrecked
Cut down to the bare bone
No. Left to drown, instead I learned to swim—
not against but with the salted ocean tides
to find my way back
home

Boneyard

You'll eat my words
and I'll spit out a trail of dust,
or diamonds
for you to walk upon.
My poems are your bones
The pointed star of your embrace
What, should I go blazing forth
into the night?
No, mine is more a quiet light

Things I Never Told You

Every love poem points its fingers at someone:
Mine are like letters mailed with just the return address

They keep getting sent back

Time is a Pool

You held me in an ecstasy of pleasure,
a shivering of our bodies together;
I wanted the world, spun, to taste of sugar
and candy
Instead, your mouth opens wordlessly
under mine
My head is a clock, its insides whirling
and I can tell you holding my hands open
that it is finally time to go

Leaving

Leaving is the worst—the breaking open
of spirits, drunk and gone, holding out over
the handles of time, holding it like a trunk
wasting time, beating time, killing time
no wonder it flies from us

Aftermath

The latticework of light
cast from the window touches your face
the way I won't and instead
I swallow hard—
a small sound that nonetheless
drops deep into the silence

Forever

She says it falteringly, as if not quite sure
what the word means in this context.
But I know better: I remember chasing darkness
like a thrill—how I branded myself with your forevers,
tattooed myself with your scars.
How you saw it all and still let me starve

Forgetting

Sleep to dream of the blank buzzing spaces
between pearled strings of memories,
as the stupefied moon casts its light like a net.
Or, I sleep to dream the dream my sister had of us dying,
her driving us off of a cliff, me in the passenger seat—
to fall screaming into nothingness
as I had dreamed so many times before.

Philomela 2.8

When you slam me against the roof of the car I see stars.
The anger I feel is decidedly un-
feminine.

Driving fast, cutting reckless corners, you
teach me how to use my fists. Yes, I was running with the fast kids;
choking back the heated exchange, regurgitated words

venomous, backward as bile. I was not afraid—I was so afraid
of the tangled dichotomy
of my anatomy.

While separate darknesses
have their own distinct sense of allure, I am no Philomel,
you cannot cut my tongue out of my gaping head.

I'll still be here.
Waiting, writing, unfolding. You can have my body,
but you cannot have my voice

Dust

We accumulate tragedy
in the same way that we shed skin;
atrophying into dust—slowly and sometimes,
without even noticing

The Thing about Loneliness

Loneliness hurts with one hand
and soothes with the other; like picking at a scab
or tonguing blood in the back of the mouth, its pull
is irresistible. Like a child, it beckons, it wheedles—
and, like the exhausted parent,
snaps back. It berates.

But that's the thing about loneliness,
because just when you think it's got you
under its skin, it, too, shuts the door behind it.
It, too, is just like all the rest:
Leaving you alone once again.

The Extremities

Maybe if we could love ourselves
with the ferocity we use to self-destruct
We would set the world afire with our love

Our desire
As we emerge from the ashes
clean, pure, more than a little confused
and alive and awake and aware
as ever

Love Letter to the World

They told me to let go of my anger
Purge the past
Well, I never was a very good bulimic
Always preferred the all-or-nothing approach
So what'll it be, dust or ash?
One day you will know
the corroded edges of my past—
They have not given me scars
They have given me
wings

Sylvia

I held hands with your ghost
all through my seventeen,
guided by your words, a balm to my corroded soul

Take me through the crushing tides of seventeen
A deep and sumptuous thing, this cake you fed me
Normally I would spit it back out—

the sugared decadence of a thousand years
of patriarchy. But Anne said, *They took you from me*
With all the bells ringing

Poetess

It's after you stop looking that you are ready to find
your Self. Losing your mind
might just be another part of the process.

What you have lost will make its way back to you,
if you let it. But remember not to forget
how it really happened.

I once told you that I found their jet-black
beautiful; spilling my soul on the stairs
overlooking the ocean. You threw your head back,

laughed—said cruelly that you'd shoot them all.
I knew you were wrong. See?
The crows will always find their way back home

Wishing Well Heart

A secret kept for years.
An unlocked door, left swinging on its hinges.
Finally, you are allowed an entrance;
finally, you are deemed worthy.

The importance of being vulnerable:
A lesson I want to teach the world, and a lesson you taught me.

A box—several boxes—full of darkness.
I am awaiting their delivery. I am absorbed in the waiting,

like people counting coins at a laundromat.
The smell of cigarette smoke a reminder
of the press and pull of the material world.

The shifting between drags, so subtle you would not even realize
that it's there—were you not paying careful attention.

You are not like them. Do not try to be.
Every second spent fighting the truth of your Self
is a waste of the time you've been given.

Remember: You are made of atoms and stardust,
and one day you will find someone
whose eyes match the constellations in your soul.

For now, there is only you—the secrets kept and revealed.
The give and take of love and loneliness. The taste of it, coppery,

like coins clinking into machines at a laundromat.
Winking back at you from the bottom of a wishing well.

(He)art & Soul

So what should you do?
Laugh a little too loudly. Love a little too hard.
Make it messy.

Fill your world with color: Paint. Play. Trip.
Splash it with prisms of light, with great bright
heaving rainbows of it. Shatter it with pink, purple, blue,

dark moody reds and sunny yellows. Green.
Vibrant, living, breathing green—your favorite,
your teeming beauteous bouquet of technicolor.

Throw it against the wall and leave it. Watch
ribbons of color drip down. Brick red. Cobalt. Mauve.
Burnt orange. Matte plum. Emerald green. Pastel pink.

Bright, sunny, chatty yellow and its equally loquacious
periwinkle blue. And when you feel like you don't fit,
when there's fear and self-judgment and discomfort,

when your soul itches—know this:
There's a door that needs to be opened.
(And if there's no door, open the fucking window.)

So, what should you do? Smile sweet and cradle your vices.
Go forth and conquer, babe—stomp and clomp
and make your presence known.

Doesn't it feel good not to be like the rest of them,
darling? It's what long ago had me dancing
on the precipice—and has saved me, again and again

and again, from the deep-seated, integral
unraveling of my own Self. So I continue on,
shouldering my bittersweets, riding high on twenty-

five. And I love it, even when it threatens to consume
me. Love it even more so, because.
What else remains?

Mythwork

The Garden

In the beginning, everything was bright in paradise:
Bathed in sweat, Eve and Adam made love in the tangled
garden. Afterward, Eve was hungry. Her stomach was a live
animal coiled inside a drum. Ravenous, she climbed a gnarled
tree in the center of the garden and sat huddled in its
branches, her body small beneath the grip
of her hands, all bones and angles.
Hunger making her wince.

An apple hung in the corner of her vision.
She could not believe how her body hurt—aching,
cringing. She took the apple. Afterward, Adam's fury
matched that previous hunger, the first carnal rage. He could
not know Eve's control, the way she maneuvered power over
a body she was told wasn't hers, that was really his.
His voice thunderous, that rage guiding his hand
like a whip cracked across her face, blinding. The pain
as if she was being beaten from the inside.
Her body self-destructing.

They needed no God to destroy them,
to cast them as unwilling pariahs into the desert
beyond the garden so that they became hopelessly lost,
unable to find paradise again.
They needed no God to destroy them:
They were perfectly capable of it themselves.

Memento

A long time ago I began to lift off from the ground,
    growing lighter and lighter with each step.

Cigarette blazing a trail through my body,
I slowly lose sight of gravity. I forget that I can't fly.

Your monstrous mouth reveals a god with his hands full of light.
And we watch, hair smashed with grief, hooking sighs

    in the curves of our mouths as dirty skies stream
upside-down lives. Once I held a book bound with moonlight,

its spine ever-shifting, palmed old Polaroid photos of a girl
    with tufted green hair and glowing opiate eyes.

Small and immense, this: My body's nebulous rebellion,
    caught spiraling in a dexterity of fingerprints and lies.

I can rip myself asunder in twenty seconds or less, want to watch?
I've planted meteorites in the garden, and I can feel the bones

    of the sea as she rolls her hips into the shore—
    counting each lovely, treacherous vertebrae.

We hop fences to sit on golf courses as the sky yawns overhead,
    blinking its one great eye. I walk with you in dreams,

holding your hand like flowers. There's a volcano growing
    in our backyard. But the world maintains its grip,

and so we slice it open like an animal to reveal its insides—
bloodwork laid out on the autumn hills.

Though the heavy pull of the ground can hardly compare
to the abrupt, insistent cage of my own Self,

and I laugh at the thought.
Brambles for skin, your mouth sprouts chrysanthemums,

now that it's almost spring. I know that time is a cage, a dream.
The trees have all put their dresses back on, and I am riding

in a car by myself into a world I can't yet see.
It's only until I feel better, you understand.

Fantastic Orgasmic Phantasm

You go along, shedding selves like skin.
Tragic events hang like keys jangling
in the inner pockets of your coat.
You dream of strange headless creatures
with wings—they wear rainbows for dresses,
eat nebulous stars like cake.
Cramming their mouths full, they pin butterflies,
labyrinthine constellations to their hair—
they get pieces of sky stuck in their teeth.
And they ask, "Why would you want to be a real girl
when you can be a fantasy instead?"
Spinning in a disillusioned mess,
one great galactic laser beam.
You hear those creatures shriek, they scream
Alighting on your head,
wanting to swallow all your memories
So you press play, go on trying to pretend
that all the dust and all the stars and all the poems
in your soul can so easily come back to life
beneath your skin

Mythwork

I do not miss the hurting:
Rows of empty-chested, hollow-faced men.
Marching on graphite walls,
I studied poetry, literature, the workings
of myth. Sat through class after class
scribbling unfinished novels in notebooks
without yet realizing
the effortless expression
the waiting
the way you can play with words like toys
I am the lines between Keats and Kerouac
We are the moments between
and I play with seconds
like eternities

The Warrior

Like some beribboned, jewel-encrusted savage
looking everywhere he could,
all of his forevers spent running away—

until finally the day comes when he looks upon himself
and sees, (fingers, rings glinting with gold,
armbands of copper and ruby-plated armor,

tendrils of gold clinging to braids that click
as he tosses his hair, chomping at the bit like some
champion-bred Thoroughbred, suddenly all too aware

of his own power)
I have always been a warrior.
Writer. Poetess. Mermaid. Hurricane.

Like some savage Odysseus,
come home after storms of running away
from himself, from love;

welding a light into many separate darknesses
separated by years, even decades; trying to find ecstasy
in odyssey—to discover in all the travels

and exploits the world has to offer, that truth which
could only be found
in the arms of the woman he loved.

The Loom

I had always thought I was Penelope
Waiting, years of faithfully
weaving and unweaving my loom

When all the time I was Odysseus
Forever licking my wounds
but stung: Coaxed by adrenaline

addicted to the adventure
of wit, of creation, of poetry,
of a world that could be

spun shining, leaping into myth

Mr. Rilke

No one is more selfish than the dead
in their leaving: Monstrous abandonment, and that pure,
floating elation. That bloodless face, shown through the

cheek and the lip; no longer human.
You turn your back to me, and you leave.
Nothing is worse than the leaving.

There is nothing more monstrous, more scarred,
than that. I longed for sleep and fell into it like a storm.
I slept the sleep of the dead.

On awakening! I felt more alive than I had ever been,
more light, more pure; I was an empty decanter,
and I had known its incessant hunger.

Its clear and ringing glass. Pure, sweet oxygen;
I breathed it in as a lover would, the smell of your hair,
the feel of your body.

Move closer inside—see what it is like, the shape of your heart,
the press of your lips. The curve of your trembling thighs.
See: Life, in its extremities of desire. Its lows.

Death like an ocean—throw yourself into its water and after,
you find yourself rising like steam, rising through it like sleep,
and you see yourself suddenly heavy.

Pressing into the sides of the world as if they were doors.
In a book you read as a child a girl fell into a well.
It led into another world.

This, you know like the back of your hand.

Aries Chrysomallus

I grew up candy-coated in the deceptive California sun.
The horns grew in while I slept one night,
hard and strangely illustrious:

Though I woke with no surprise to see them press carefully out
from beneath a head wild with dreams, curls like flying away.

They grow down all pretty, see, how they wink with light?
And the golden coat my mother gave me
is perfect for tonight's party.

When I pull it on, I push my fingers into the comforting fleece
and put my hooves on like a badge of fucking honor.

My anger is so pretty, see? Promise.
Watch me curl my lashes with it
like mascara. The sky is calling,

and I'm thirsty—having long since eloped
with thoughts of my own recklessness. And the ram?

She cornered me long ago,
brought her head and horns down.
Nose powdered, prepped for the slaughter.

I'm still wearing her golden coat.
Now I run out in the street,

clutching great cosmic stitches in my stomach.

They implode, erupt. Why don't they know that to be female
means to be a volcano?

We give birth to the world, again and again.
Why do they try to take it from us?

Icarus

You give me your watch,
then turn and deck a stranger in the face.
When I look down, I'm surprised to see the glint of
gold peeking between my palms—I'm clutching the strap
so hard it lays a heavy indentation in the skin of my hand. But
this goes unnoticed as you dart down a street quick with the flow
of moving bodies, and I hitch the strap of my purse tight
against my side as the rest of us pelt after you.
Gasping, as if directed by the pull of some
great gravitational force.

I know this: You want to be close to the sun.
Your erratic movements, the constant, volatile tug
of your anger—you find pleasure in the violence of it.
All your life, you've never cared who has to burn
just for you to stay warm.

The Arena

Tonguing copper secrets like blood
in the back of your mouth, you arrive on
winged platform shoes, tumble into an arena
where the only thing they allow you to

arm yourself with is words.
So you calmly stockpile every book you've ever read,
pile memories into your pockets, poems curling
around your neck. They coil and hiss beneath

your hair, Medusa's snakes darting to eat
their own heads. (And there's still such a swooping
pleasure in this torturous game—can you swallow
the sword of your own self-loathing? Can you make

'em all stare? Will it be worth it?)
You chop your own head off, laughingly add it
to the growing number you juggle. You are a Medusa
of your own making—and the crowd fucking loves it.

Desire is singularly distracting, you see,
especially when memories coat your pockets.
Watch: As you slide scraps from them, your skin
turns to paper, glows translucent,

veins marking their careful place with ink.
Now if only you could remember what you're

remembering to forget. You must know
that the demons in the arena

grinning back at you cannot be your redemption.
Self-hate isn't a rebellion. It's a sacrifice.
And what had you ever truly loved, then,
if it wasn't to rebel?

So you fist your hands into your pockets,
come away with this one last poem, everything
else long gone. All you have, now, is this:
The knowledge that a poem is not like a song or a story

but instead stripped down to the bones,
the very soul of something.
I write it all down so that I won't forget;
I told you that before you went in.

Because this is what we strive to remember:
Not that impossible eventuality of loss,
but those remembrances of humankind
falling in love with itself. Again and again and again.

So that when you shred yourself down
to those last scraps of paper,
those last couple words, and let
your head drop to roll—you won't die.

So that when the crowd sets each other ablaze,
they won't either. And though the arena still beckons—
we can instead say, look what we made.
What better weapon to arm ourselves with?

Keeping the Light

Entropy

Emptiness glitters—

Moon Skin

I have known what it is to be made ugly, blackened
by the imprint of you—erased, imprisoned, embalmed.

Like the moon serene and whole from afar,
but on closer look skin made imperfect by the scars of her

craters, her rocks. I soak myself in her lit up gaze,
drink the night sky in, gulp the stars…always

thirsty for more.
The constellations spill like bloodwine from my glass,

imperceptibly hovering out of reach.
Like you as you walk away,

watching the moon from the
corner of your eye as if she'll chase you.

(the way I never
did)

or maybe, just maybe
as if she'll guide you

on your way home.

Deep Sea Diving

Hope drifts away, cradling the smoke from your cigarette.
You tap the ash out over the gutter;
you swallow noisily and begin to walk.

Your chest feels heavier with every step, like a trunk being filled
and refilled with gold—each clinking coin.

When you look in the mirror, your eyes are as empty as these
lantern-bright mirages. Can this be you? You are a stranger to

yourself. Yet you still hug her against the cold,
and you still speak to her as if
she is worthy—in the rain, you reassure her:

There's an overhang nearby.
Home is close to here. There are friends there.
There will be food, and drink.

You write a book, never putting down your cigarette.
The ashtray begs to be used, screams for fulfillment.

You do not touch it.
You will not give in.
Watch this: the television's light flickers bluely on.

You are deep under the sea. The ocean's longing sings to you,
its waves humming. The memory of each caress lit from within,

fogged up from the inside, as if lanterns hang beneath.

You briefly consider writing him a letter,
and then toss the cigarette away.

Crystalline

The crystal glows with multi-faceted iridescence,
throwing off pointed shadows, sharp reflections
like the recesses of a vast canyon.
Your eyes an echo.

The purity of the rock absolves sin, all emotion,
even love. Angelite. Calcite. Citrine. Quartz.
Black sparkling tourmaline.
Pyrite winking false.

I like the way their names roll coolly on my tongue,
like the stones themselves. Like picturing rose quartz
with its pinked cheeks, another weary housewife,
worn-down love stone.

Onyx, roiling black spirit;
even it can be rubbed to smoothness in time,
proof of elemental ferocity, rubbed away—
left wanting, simply, for salt.

This one in particular: amethyst, its presence still,
temporal, gathered in my small brown palms. Chrysalis.
Just a moment, left to cut through shafts of dust.
Perfumed by sorrow,

the shifting of blood that precedes a storm of longing,
and yet, it is a pleasing testament to worldly permanence—

or maybe it's opposite. I want in that instant
to make my heart hard.

As diamond. As pure.
Instead I am flint before the striking,
mere seconds before immolation.
No, I am shattered sea-glass,

jagged purple, green, then rust-colored shards.
The glass cuts my hands, but the blood doesn't
spill when it reaches air: Instead it
sings

And the stone? A secret loosely kept for years,
like your hand in my pocket. Careful.
A shock of intimacy
that quietly glows.

Gold Souled

Heavy footsteps tread against a map of the night.
Borne into pinpricks of brilliance, and the vast silence
of reproachful stars. Soft, faded maps. A slowly spinning globe.
Weave your hands into the texture of my soul.

Sew yourself into the sea of my constellations,
star-studded sky and planets, the rising tides, the ebb and flow.
Passion drips liquid gold along my legs, the landscape
of a canyon, behind my eyes, my lively bloodstream.

Like a moon, my love caught in the orbit of your affection.
Dip your head to kiss the stars clinging to my lips, as on and on
beyond its grasp, you see my hands forever reach and then—
we wrench ourselves away, gasping.

A soul isn't smooth as one would think; instead it's chunky,
rocky in some places, frayed where sadness sucks at its edges.
Pieces of art get stuck on the ends. It goes through
long periods of darkness before lighting up again.

Stardust

Crescent moon like a startle of teeth just before
it rips through the mouth of the sky. Sometimes I hide my face
from the sun, finding solace in this pearled, baby teeth moon.
My heart tucks itself away, seeking comfort, a small slice of safety.
Looking for someone or something to hold its hand
in the dusty corners of this dark place.

Supernova

Darkness is not the opposite of light, merely the absence
and you were always so good at disappearing
You come, bleeding darkness, with a lantern in one hand
and a tennis racket in the other
Sometimes I think I was a supernova in a past life
I carried the light, once—wretched Prometheus

Metamorphosis

I have always found it to be achingly beautiful
the way that stars are strung, sparkling lights
hung from empty space, sitting pretty
on a galactic swing. They die a thousand deaths
just to reach us as our bodies touch,
casting warmth and wet against the flatline—
only to come away again. Like the serpent
eating its own head, like the sound
the sky makes in November:
Remember that a snake must itch
before it sheds its skin

Seacliff

A spray of mist, light dew, and your cancerous love
atop the sea cliffs. I have no wish to be anything but—
the scorpion's barb, venomous. We marvel that something
so small should be so deadly, watch as rock formations
rise and give way. Glaciers bow down deep. Rifts in the earth
yawn like tattooed flesh, wrinkles worn in the grooves.
And a record that keeps playing, its small sigh circuitous.
Where does it come from? 5 AM, 6. Where does it go?

Messy

You need someone calmer, tamer—
someone who isn't ruled by their passions
and their poetry, someone who won't retreat
like a vanishing tide when the moon turns her
face. So? You don't need me, but I do.
I need my Self now more than ever—
and I'm so glad I found me.

Belong

Now that I'm my own,
(fully and wonderfully and cosmically,
wildly and tumultuously, intrinsically
and whimsically my own),
we both know that
you'll never
have me
again

Ghoul City

Cloaked with fog like the bristling fur
of a great silvered beast. Heaving hills, the city rises—
its skyline riddled with pockmarks. Succulents crowd
the street corners, bougainvillea curls upward
into clouded-over skies. In this city, one can spin tales
of their own darkness into weapons, to wield them
against the demons of their own making.
She rides her dreams like winged horses
through another tempestuous San Francisco night.
Los Angeles tastes like talc in the mouth, smoggy
cotton candy sunsets every night, as toxic chem trails
trace arcs of danger across the sky. A corrupt kind of beauty,
the most dangerous in its deception. Because the only thing
she's ever really been good at, aside from penning
a pretty line of poetry, is an accelerated
personal entropy—and the thing I seek
is so much less easily attainable
than the haphazard love of another human being.
But San Francisco doesn't lie. She preens, peacock pretty.
So we live on, tearing into our nerve endings,
in the deep, worn vicissitudes of our own extremes:
Our nostrils cave in. Our hearts slowly wither.
But we take glittering solace in the fact
that we will never be like them, and in that—
we are free.

Immolation

You carry the light with you.
You carry it through
Peeking through the basket weave
Dizzying still
Leaking light, spilling it
Like the emptiness
not before a fire starts but just after
it burns out

Scribbles

If everything was so small I could wear the Universe
like a dress, slide it over my legs thighs hipbones waist breasts
and it clung like rain, pearling my hair and neck
would you sew my words into my skin

so that I'd never die?
The world's a mess, you know that;
small children eat it for breakfast. But still I go cartwheeling
through the cosmos. I am a constitution of stars, messy,

I vomit them like neon parasites. I think in spirals,
giggle sartorial secrets. And in the morning I still get up
and tie my hair back, play with the sun like a golden cat.
So that when we dance, it's in galaxies spun-over with folded light,

the room mirrored with prismatic speckles
against the walls, multidimensional shards of heaven.
My heart is a wounded animal, and I am mysterious
even unto myself. I create something from nothing,

and to you that is its own kind of redemption.
To me, it is sanctuary.
I'll be reciting poetry on my deathbed.
Come listen.

The Gloaming

You are not your darkness. You are not your pain. You are not the part of you that finds it hard to get out of bed in the morning—but the part that does it anyway. You are the pieces of a heart that's been broken, but managed to survive. You are vast bells ringing. You are the universe dreaming. You are the transforming.

Keeping the Light

The ocean scares me far more
than deep space. Its pressures, its intricacies—
its creatures. And yet, within a spiral of nebulas,
I sit, anxiously pressing two pieces of wire together.
Chasing, coaxing, keeping the light
as I hide between the holes,
smear the gaps between atoms—
and hover in the shimmering blankness
between worlds. I am a conglomerate
of separate darknesses. I am the empty spaces
between everything. But I will be more than that.
I will carry you on my back. I will carry you
with me.

The Luminary

The moon drips velvet and the night,
it breathes hot as your breath behind my ear.
A thousand sunsets rim my glass;
what mischievous alchemy.
How strange it is to realize after all this time
My soul has lived a thousand lives,
told a thousand stories,
sailed into the vast and mysterious night sky
to navigate a thousand nights without you.
I have dreamed countless lives,
been battered and worn, been reborn.
In one past life I was a rotting star,
in another a black hole.
Now I search the dark places, but I am not alone.
I am the world and the world is inside my chest.

About the Author

By day, Kimia Madani is a writer based in San Francisco, California. By night, she dreams of chasing the silvery cloud banks that hang above her favorite city and spinning in long, unhurried circles on the moon. With a name that means alchemy among other things, she believes in writing to escape, define, and reinvent the exhilarating design of her own world. Also in the power of green hair and holographic shoes. Find her on Instagram @kkimbunny.

YOU MIGHT ALSO LIKE:

All The Words I Should Have Said by Rania Naim

Seeds Planted in Concrete by Bianca Sparacino

Bloodline by Ari Eastman

THOUGHT
CATALOG
Books